MW01235120

GRATITUDE IS A MUST
BE GRATEFUL EVERYDAY

This Gratitude Journal Belongs to

_____

WHAT IS A GRATITUDE JOURNAL?

Gratulations! You have taken the first step towards a better you!

In life, we tend to focus more on all the things that are not working for us instead of looking at all the things that have been working. All the blessings that is behind and in front of you. That's what a gratitude journal does. Each day you wake up you remind yourself of all the things that have been working in your life and throughout the day you are consciously counting your blessings. This allows you to focus on only positive influences, therefore impacting the law of attraction.

Whether you think you can, or you think you can't, you are right. When you focus on positive thoughts you will become aware of how good you are and how blessed you are to wake up daily. You will gain more self-confidence, extend yourself more to others, stop feeling sorry for yourself, be more courageous and have more faith in yourself.

Throughout this journal I have incorporated law of attraction and gratitude quotes that you can reflect on daily. I have also added a list of items that you can be thankful for.

Spend at least 3 days each week reflecting on the things that you are grateful for. Add notes on the notes page. Make plans to change your life and watch your life change accordingly, Oprah Winfrey used the strategy and she is a millionaire.

Sincerely Yours,
Yanique Walters-Dynott
@gratitudeisamust

HOW DOES A GRATITUDE JOURNAL WORK?

When you count your blessings its boosts both your happiness and well-being. Being grateful has shown to improve many aspects of one's life. It makes you sleep better at nights, build your self-esteem, better relationships with others and will help you to be more resilient.

Each day choose a time that works for you. Start out by writing down 5 things you are grateful for at the start of the day and as the day go by, add things that happened that made you even more grateful.

For example, noticing a car accident 2 cars before you. This is something for you to be grateful for because that could have been you. While you might be sad about the persons involved, you also must give thanks and be grateful that you are still alive.

Each day write a list of people you are grateful for. This list might repeat daily, however, I advise that each day you think outside the box and think about people that made you smile, that helped you with something while you were out and about, maybe your coworker did something to make your day better. These are the kind of things you want to include in your list of people and not just the default, mom, dad, siblings, spouse.

You also want to make your list specific. Instead of saying you are grateful for food, say what food you were grateful for on that specific day. For example, instead of saying Cheese Cake, you can say the delicious Cheese Cake at Devon's House.

Add additional notes on the notes page as you go and always remember to update your grateful journal.

When you stop complaining about the things you don't have and start focusing on the things you do have, you start to appreciate life more which ultimately improves the quality of your life!

What are you waiting on? Start today!

"Every single second is an opportunity to change your life, because in any moment you can change the way you feel."

RHONDA BYRNE

LET'S BE GRATEFUL!

Day........................... Month........................... Year...........................

LIST 5 THINGS YOU ARE GRATEFUL FOR TODAY.

(Before doing anything today, reflect on things that you wake up feeling grateful about.)

1
2
3
4
5

WHAT DID YOU LEARN TODAY?

(What did you learn from your challenges today? What positive lesson came from the day?)

1
2
3
4
5

PEOPLE YOU ARE GRATEFUL FOR?

(Reflect on those people that made your day a happy one, or showed you support and list them.)

1
2
3
4
5

THE BEST PART OF YOUR DAY?

(Before you go to bed, think about what part of your day made you happy and reflect on it.)

1
2
3
4
5

SOMETHING FUN THAT YOU ARE LOOKING FORWARD TO?

My Thoughts

LET'S BE GRATEFUL!

Day......................... Month........................... Year.........................

LIST 5 THINGS YOU ARE GRATEFUL FOR TODAY.

(Before doing anything today, reflect on things that you wake up feeling grateful about.)

1
2
3
4
5

WHAT DID YOU LEARN TODAY?

(What did you learn from your challenges today? What positive lesson came from the day?)

1
2
3
4
5

PEOPLE YOU ARE GRATEFUL FOR?

(Reflect on those people that made your day a happy one, or showed you support and list them.)

1
2
3
4
5

THE BEST PART OF YOUR DAY?

(Before you go to bed, think about what part of your day made you happy and reflect on it.)

1
2
3
4
5

SOMETHING FUN THAT YOU ARE LOOKING FORWARD TO?

My Thoughts

LET'S BE GRATEFUL!

Day........................ Month........................ Year........................

LIST 5 THINGS YOU ARE GRATEFUL FOR TODAY.

(Before doing anything today, reflect on things that you wake up feeling grateful about.)

1
2
3
4
5

WHAT DID YOU LEARN TODAY?

(What did you learn from your challenges today? What positive lesson came from the day?)

1
2
3
4
5

PEOPLE YOU ARE GRATEFUL FOR?

(Reflect on those people that made your day a happy one, or showed you support and list them.)

1
2
3
4
5

THE BEST PART OF YOUR DAY?

(Before you go to bed, think about what part of your day made you happy and reflect on it.)

1
2
3
4
5

SOMETHING FUN THAT YOU ARE LOOKING FORWARD TO?

My Thoughts

"Every morning when I open my curtains for that first look at the day, no matter what the day looks like—raining, foggy, overcast, sunny— my heart swells with gratitude. I get another chance.

OPRAH WINFREY

LET'S BE GRATEFUL!

Day......................... Month........................... Year..........................

LIST 5 THINGS YOU ARE GRATEFUL FOR TODAY.

(Before doing anything today, reflect on things that you wake up feeling grateful about.)

1
2
3
4
5

WHAT DID YOU LEARN TODAY?

(What did you learn from your challenges today? What positive lesson came from the day?)

1
2
3
4
5

PEOPLE YOU ARE GRATEFUL FOR?

(Reflect on those people that made your day a happy one, or showed you support and list them.)

1
2
3
4
5

THE BEST PART OF YOUR DAY?

(Before you go to bed, think about what part of your day made you happy and reflect on it.)

1
2
3
4
5

SOMETHING FUN THAT YOU ARE LOOKING FORWARD TO?

My Thoughts

LET'S BE GRATEFUL!

Day........................... Month........................... Year...........................

LIST 5 THINGS YOU ARE GRATEFUL FOR TODAY.

(Before doing anything today, reflect on things that you wake up feeling grateful about.)

1
2
3
4
5

WHAT DID YOU LEARN TODAY?

(What did you learn from your challenges today? What positive lesson came from the day?)

1
2
3
4
5

PEOPLE YOU ARE GRATEFUL FOR?

(Reflect on those people that made your day a happy one, or showed you support and list them.)

1
2
3
4
5

THE BEST PART OF YOUR DAY?

(Before you go to bed, think about what part of your day made you happy and reflect on it.)

1
2
3
4
5

SOMETHING FUN THAT YOU ARE LOOKING FORWARD TO?

My Thoughts

LET'S BE GRATEFUL!

Day......................... Month........................... Year.........................

LIST 5 THINGS YOU ARE GRATEFUL FOR TODAY.

(Before doing anything today, reflect on things that you wake up feeling grateful about.)

1
2
3
4
5

WHAT DID YOU LEARN TODAY?

(What did you learn from your challenges today? What positive lesson came from the day?)

1
2
3
4
5

PEOPLE YOU ARE GRATEFUL FOR?

(Reflect on those people that made your day a happy one, or showed you support and list them.)

1
2
3
4
5

THE BEST PART OF YOUR DAY?

(Before you go to bed, think about what part of your day made you happy and reflect on it.)

1
2
3
4
5

SOMETHING FUN THAT YOU ARE LOOKING FORWARD TO?

My Thoughts

"Every single second is an opportunity to change your life, because in any moment you can change the way you feel."

RHONDA BYRNE

LET'S BE GRATEFUL!

Day......................... Month.......................... Year..........................

LIST 5 THINGS YOU ARE GRATEFUL FOR TODAY.

(Before doing anything today, reflect on things that you wake up feeling grateful about.)

1
2
3
4
5

WHAT DID YOU LEARN TODAY?

(What did you learn from your challenges today? What positive lesson came from the day?)

1
2
3
4
5

PEOPLE YOU ARE GRATEFUL FOR?

(Reflect on those people that made your day a happy one, or showed you support and list them.)

1
2
3
4
5

THE BEST PART OF YOUR DAY?

(Before you go to bed, think about what part of your day made you happy and reflect on it.)

1
2
3
4
5

SOMETHING FUN THAT YOU ARE LOOKING FORWARD TO?

My Thoughts

LET'S BE GRATEFUL!

Day........................... Month........................... Year...........................

LIST 5 THINGS YOU ARE GRATEFUL FOR TODAY.

(Before doing anything today, reflect on things that you wake up feeling grateful about.)

1
2
3
4
5

WHAT DID YOU LEARN TODAY?

(What did you learn from your challenges today? What positive lesson came from the day?)

1
2
3
4
5

PEOPLE YOU ARE GRATEFUL FOR?

(Reflect on those people that made your day a happy one, or showed you support and list them.)

1
2
3
4
5

THE BEST PART OF YOUR DAY?

(Before you go to bed, think about what part of your day made you happy and reflect on it.)

1
2
3
4
5

SOMETHING FUN THAT YOU ARE LOOKING FORWARD TO?

My Thoughts

LET'S BE GRATEFUL!

Day......................... Month......................... Year.........................

LIST 5 THINGS YOU ARE GRATEFUL FOR TODAY.

(Before doing anything today, reflect on things that you wake up feeling grateful about.)

1
2
3
4
5

WHAT DID YOU LEARN TODAY?

(What did you learn from your challenges today? What positive lesson came from the day?)

1
2
3
4
5

PEOPLE YOU ARE GRATEFUL FOR?

(Reflect on those people that made your day a happy one, or showed you support and list them.)

1
2
3
4
5

THE BEST PART OF YOUR DAY?

(Before you go to bed, think about what part of your day made you happy and reflect on it.)

1
2
3
4
5

SOMETHING FUN THAT YOU ARE LOOKING FORWARD TO?

My Thoughts

"It is the combination of thought and love which forms the irresistible force of the law of attraction."

CHARLES HAMMEL

LET'S BE GRATEFUL!

Day.......................... Month.......................... Year..........................

LIST 5 THINGS YOU ARE GRATEFUL FOR TODAY.

(Before doing anything today, reflect on things that you wake up feeling grateful about.)

1
2
3
4
5

WHAT DID YOU LEARN TODAY?

(What did you learn from your challenges today? What positive lesson came from the day?)

1
2
3
4
5

PEOPLE YOU ARE GRATEFUL FOR?

(Reflect on those people that made your day a happy one, or showed you support and list them.)

1
2
3
4
5

THE BEST PART OF YOUR DAY?

(Before you go to bed, think about what part of your day made you happy and reflect on it.)

1
2
3
4
5

SOMETHING FUN THAT YOU ARE LOOKING FORWARD TO?

My Thoughts

LET'S BE GRATEFUL!

Day........................ Month............................ Year..........................

LIST 5 THINGS YOU ARE GRATEFUL FOR TODAY.

(Before doing anything today, reflect on things that you wake up feeling grateful about.)

1
2
3
4
5

WHAT DID YOU LEARN TODAY?

(What did you learn from your challenges today? What positive lesson came from the day?)

1
2
3
4
5

PEOPLE YOU ARE GRATEFUL FOR?

(Reflect on those people that made your day a happy one, or showed you support and list them.)

1
2
3
4
5

THE BEST PART OF YOUR DAY?

(Before you go to bed, think about what part of your day made you happy and reflect on it.)

1
2
3
4
5

SOMETHING FUN THAT YOU ARE LOOKING FORWARD TO?

My Thoughts

LET'S BE GRATEFUL!

Day........................... Month............................ Year...........................

LIST 5 THINGS YOU ARE GRATEFUL FOR TODAY.

(Before doing anything today, reflect on things that you wake up feeling grateful about.)

1
2
3
4
5

WHAT DID YOU LEARN TODAY?

(What did you learn from your challenges today? What positive lesson came from the day?)

1
2
3
4
5

PEOPLE YOU ARE GRATEFUL FOR?

(Reflect on those people that made your day a happy one, or showed you support and list them.)

1
2
3
4
5

THE BEST PART OF YOUR DAY?

(Before you go to bed, think about what part of your day made you happy and reflect on it.)

1
2
3
4
5

SOMETHING FUN THAT YOU ARE LOOKING FORWARD TO?

My Thoughts

" See the things that you want as already yours. Know that they will come to you at need. Then let them come. Don't fret and worry about them. Don't think about your lack of them. Think of them as yours, as belonging to you, as already in your possession."

ROBERT COLLIER

LET'S BE GRATEFUL!

Day.......................... Month........................... Year...........................

LIST 5 THINGS YOU ARE GRATEFUL FOR TODAY.

(Before doing anything today, reflect on things that you wake up feeling grateful about.)

1
2
3
4
5

WHAT DID YOU LEARN TODAY?

(What did you learn from your challenges today? What positive lesson came from the day?)

1
2
3
4
5

PEOPLE YOU ARE GRATEFUL FOR?

(Reflect on those people that made your day a happy one, or showed you support and list them.)

1
2
3
4
5

THE BEST PART OF YOUR DAY?

(Before you go to bed, think about what part of your day made you happy and reflect on it.)

1
2
3
4
5

SOMETHING FUN THAT YOU ARE LOOKING FORWARD TO?

My Thoughts

LET'S BE GRATEFUL!

Day.......................... Month........................... Year...........................

LIST 5 THINGS YOU ARE GRATEFUL FOR TODAY.

(Before doing anything today, reflect on things that you wake up feeling grateful about.)

1
2
3
4
5

WHAT DID YOU LEARN TODAY?

(What did you learn from your challenges today? What positive lesson came from the day?)

1
2
3
4
5

PEOPLE YOU ARE GRATEFUL FOR?

(Reflect on those people that made your day a happy one, or showed you support and list them.)

1
2
3
4
5

THE BEST PART OF YOUR DAY?

(Before you go to bed, think about what part of your day made you happy and reflect on it.)

1
2
3
4
5

SOMETHING FUN THAT YOU ARE LOOKING FORWARD TO?

My Thoughts

LET'S BE GRATEFUL!

Day........................... Month........................... Year...........................

LIST 5 THINGS YOU ARE GRATEFUL FOR TODAY.

(Before doing anything today, reflect on things that you wake up feeling grateful about.)

1
2
3
4
5

WHAT DID YOU LEARN TODAY?

(What did you learn from your challenges today? What positive lesson came from the day?)

1
2
3
4
5

PEOPLE YOU ARE GRATEFUL FOR?

(Reflect on those people that made your day a happy one, or showed you support and list them.)

1
2
3
4
5

THE BEST PART OF YOUR DAY?

(Before you go to bed, think about what part of your day made you happy and reflect on it.)

1
2
3
4
5

SOMETHING FUN THAT YOU ARE LOOKING FORWARD TO?

My Thoughts

"I know for sure that only by owning who and what you are can you step into the fullness of life. I feel sorry for anyone who buys into the myth that you can be what you once were. The way to your best life isn't denial. It's owning every moment and staking a claim to the here and now… And I'm grateful for every age I'm blessed to become.

OPRAH WINFREY

LET'S BE GRATEFUL!

Day......................... Month........................... Year...........................

LIST 5 THINGS YOU ARE GRATEFUL FOR TODAY.

(Before doing anything today, reflect on things that you wake up feeling grateful about.)

1
2
3
4
5

WHAT DID YOU LEARN TODAY?

(What did you learn from your challenges today? What positive lesson came from the day?)

1
2
3
4
5

PEOPLE YOU ARE GRATEFUL FOR?

(Reflect on those people that made your day a happy one, or showed you support and list them.)

1
2
3
4
5

THE BEST PART OF YOUR DAY?

(Before you go to bed, think about what part of your day made you happy and reflect on it.)

1
2
3
4
5

SOMETHING FUN THAT YOU ARE LOOKING FORWARD TO?

My Thoughts

LET'S BE GRATEFUL!

Day.......................... Month........................... Year.........................

LIST 5 THINGS YOU ARE GRATEFUL FOR TODAY.

(Before doing anything today, reflect on things that you wake up feeling grateful about.)

1
2
3
4
5

WHAT DID YOU LEARN TODAY?

(What did you learn from your challenges today? What positive lesson came from the day?)

1
2
3
4
5

PEOPLE YOU ARE GRATEFUL FOR?

(Reflect on those people that made your day a happy one, or showed you support and list them.)

1
2
3
4
5

THE BEST PART OF YOUR DAY?

(Before you go to bed, think about what part of your day made you happy and reflect on it.)

1
2
3
4
5

SOMETHING FUN THAT YOU ARE LOOKING FORWARD TO?

My Thoughts

LET'S BE GRATEFUL!

Day........................... Month........................... Year...........................

LIST 5 THINGS YOU ARE GRATEFUL FOR TODAY.

(Before doing anything today, reflect on things that you wake up feeling grateful about.)

1
2
3
4
5

WHAT DID YOU LEARN TODAY?

(What did you learn from your challenges today? What positive lesson came from the day?)

1
2
3
4
5

PEOPLE YOU ARE GRATEFUL FOR?

(Reflect on those people that made your day a happy one, or showed you support and list them.)

1
2
3
4
5

THE BEST PART OF YOUR DAY?

(Before you go to bed, think about what part of your day made you happy and reflect on it.)

1
2
3
4
5

SOMETHING FUN THAT YOU ARE LOOKING FORWARD TO?

My Thoughts

"What things so ever ye desire, when ye pray, believe that ye receive them, and ye shall have them."

MARK 11:24

LET'S BE GRATEFUL!

Day......................... Month........................... Year...........................

LIST 5 THINGS YOU ARE GRATEFUL FOR TODAY.

(Before doing anything today, reflect on things that you wake up feeling grateful about.)

1
2
3
4
5

WHAT DID YOU LEARN TODAY?

(What did you learn from your challenges today? What positive lesson came from the day?)

1
2
3
4
5

PEOPLE YOU ARE GRATEFUL FOR?

(Reflect on those people that made your day a happy one, or showed you support and list them.)

1
2
3
4
5

THE BEST PART OF YOUR DAY?

(Before you go to bed, think about what part of your day made you happy and reflect on it.)

1
2
3
4
5

SOMETHING FUN THAT YOU ARE LOOKING FORWARD TO?

My Thoughts

LET'S BE GRATEFUL!

Day........................ Month......................... Year.........................

LIST 5 THINGS YOU ARE GRATEFUL FOR TODAY.

(Before doing anything today, reflect on things that you wake up feeling grateful about.)

1
2
3
4
5

WHAT DID YOU LEARN TODAY?

(What did you learn from your challenges today? What positive lesson came from the day?)

1
2
3
4
5

PEOPLE YOU ARE GRATEFUL FOR?

(Reflect on those people that made your day a happy one, or showed you support and list them.)

1
2
3
4
5

THE BEST PART OF YOUR DAY?

(Before you go to bed, think about what part of your day made you happy and reflect on it.)

1
2
3
4
5

SOMETHING FUN THAT YOU ARE LOOKING FORWARD TO?

My Thoughts

LET'S BE GRATEFUL!

Day......................... Month........................... Year..........................

LIST 5 THINGS YOU ARE GRATEFUL FOR TODAY.

(Before doing anything today, reflect on things that you wake up feeling grateful about.)

1
2
3
4
5

WHAT DID YOU LEARN TODAY?

(What did you learn from your challenges today? What positive lesson came from the day?)

1
2
3
4
5

PEOPLE YOU ARE GRATEFUL FOR?

(Reflect on those people that made your day a happy one, or showed you support and list them.)

1
2
3
4
5

THE BEST PART OF YOUR DAY?

(Before you go to bed, think about what part of your day made you happy and reflect on it.)

1
2
3
4
5

SOMETHING FUN THAT YOU ARE LOOKING FORWARD TO?

My Thoughts

"Take the first step in faith. You don't have to see the whole staircase. Just take the first step."

DR MARTIN LUTHER KING JR.

LET'S BE GRATEFUL!

Day......................... Month.......................... Year.........................

LIST 5 THINGS YOU ARE GRATEFUL FOR TODAY.

(Before doing anything today, reflect on things that you wake up feeling grateful about.)

1
2
3
4
5

WHAT DID YOU LEARN TODAY?

(What did you learn from your challenges today? What positive lesson came from the day?)

1
2
3
4
5

PEOPLE YOU ARE GRATEFUL FOR?

(Reflect on those people that made your day a happy one, or showed you support and list them.)

1
2
3
4
5

THE BEST PART OF YOUR DAY?

(Before you go to bed, think about what part of your day made you happy and reflect on it.)

1
2
3
4
5

SOMETHING FUN THAT YOU ARE LOOKING FORWARD TO?

My Thoughts

LET'S BE GRATEFUL!

Day........................ Month........................... Year........................

LIST 5 THINGS YOU ARE GRATEFUL FOR TODAY.

(Before doing anything today, reflect on things that you wake up feeling grateful about.)

1
2
3
4
5

WHAT DID YOU LEARN TODAY?

(What did you learn from your challenges today? What positive lesson came from the day?)

1
2
3
4
5

PEOPLE YOU ARE GRATEFUL FOR?

(Reflect on those people that made your day a happy one, or showed you support and list them.)

1
2
3
4
5

THE BEST PART OF YOUR DAY?

(Before you go to bed, think about what part of your day made you happy and reflect on it.)

1
2
3
4
5

SOMETHING FUN THAT YOU ARE LOOKING FORWARD TO?

My Thoughts

LET'S BE GRATEFUL!

Day......................... Month.......................... Year.........................

LIST 5 THINGS YOU ARE GRATEFUL FOR TODAY.

(Before doing anything today, reflect on things that you wake up feeling grateful about.)

1
2
3
4
5

WHAT DID YOU LEARN TODAY?

(What did you learn from your challenges today? What positive lesson came from the day?)

1
2
3
4
5

PEOPLE YOU ARE GRATEFUL FOR?

(Reflect on those people that made your day a happy one, or showed you support and list them.)

1
2
3
4
5

THE BEST PART OF YOUR DAY?

(Before you go to bed, think about what part of your day made you happy and reflect on it.)

1
2
3
4
5

SOMETHING FUN THAT YOU ARE LOOKING FORWARD TO?

My Thoughts

"Those who think they have no time for bodily exercises will sooner or later have to find time for illness."

EDWARD STANLEY

LET'S BE GRATEFUL!

Day.......................... Month.......................... Year..........................

LIST 5 THINGS YOU ARE GRATEFUL FOR TODAY.

(Before doing anything today, reflect on things that you wake up feeling grateful about.)

1
2
3
4
5

WHAT DID YOU LEARN TODAY?

(What did you learn from your challenges today? What positive lesson came from the day?)

1
2
3
4
5

PEOPLE YOU ARE GRATEFUL FOR?

(Reflect on those people that made your day a happy one, or showed you support and list them.)

1
2
3
4
5

THE BEST PART OF YOUR DAY?

(Before you go to bed, think about what part of your day made you happy and reflect on it.)

1
2
3
4
5

SOMETHING FUN THAT YOU ARE LOOKING FORWARD TO?

My Thoughts

LET'S BE GRATEFUL!

Day........................... Month........................... Year...........................

LIST 5 THINGS YOU ARE GRATEFUL FOR TODAY.

(Before doing anything today, reflect on things that you wake up feeling grateful about.)

1
2
3
4
5

WHAT DID YOU LEARN TODAY?

(What did you learn from your challenges today? What positive lesson came from the day?)

1
2
3
4
5

PEOPLE YOU ARE GRATEFUL FOR?

(Reflect on those people that made your day a happy one, or showed you support and list them.)

1
2
3
4
5

THE BEST PART OF YOUR DAY?

(Before you go to bed, think about what part of your day made you happy and reflect on it.)

1
2
3
4
5

SOMETHING FUN THAT YOU ARE LOOKING FORWARD TO?

My Thoughts

LET'S BE GRATEFUL!

Day............................ Month............................ Year............................

LIST 5 THINGS YOU ARE GRATEFUL FOR TODAY.

(Before doing anything today, reflect on things that you wake up feeling grateful about.)

1
2
3
4
5

WHAT DID YOU LEARN TODAY?

(What did you learn from your challenges today? What positive lesson came from the day?)

1
2
3
4
5

PEOPLE YOU ARE GRATEFUL FOR?

(Reflect on those people that made your day a happy one, or showed you support and list them.)

1
2
3
4
5

THE BEST PART OF YOUR DAY?

(Before you go to bed, think about what part of your day made you happy and reflect on it.)

1
2
3
4
5

SOMETHING FUN THAT YOU ARE LOOKING FORWARD TO?

My Thoughts

" I live in the space of thankfulness — and for that, I have been rewarded a million times over. I started out giving thanks for small things, and the more thankful I became, the more my bounty increased. That's because — for sure — what you focus on expands. When you focus on the goodness in life, you create more of it.

OPRAH WINFREY

LET'S BE GRATEFUL!

Day........................... Month........................... Year...........................

LIST 5 THINGS YOU ARE GRATEFUL FOR TODAY.

(Before doing anything today, reflect on things that you wake up feeling grateful about.)

1
2
3
4
5

WHAT DID YOU LEARN TODAY?

(What did you learn from your challenges today? What positive lesson came from the day?)

1
2
3
4
5

PEOPLE YOU ARE GRATEFUL FOR?

(Reflect on those people that made your day a happy one, or showed you support and list them.)

1
2
3
4
5

THE BEST PART OF YOUR DAY?

(Before you go to bed, think about what part of your day made you happy and reflect on it.)

1
2
3
4
5

SOMETHING FUN THAT YOU ARE LOOKING FORWARD TO?

My Thoughts

LET'S BE GRATEFUL!

Day........................ Month........................... Year...........................

LIST 5 THINGS YOU ARE GRATEFUL FOR TODAY.

(Before doing anything today, reflect on things that you wake up feeling grateful about.)

1
2
3
4
5

WHAT DID YOU LEARN TODAY?

(What did you learn from your challenges today? What positive lesson came from the day?)

1
2
3
4
5

PEOPLE YOU ARE GRATEFUL FOR?

(Reflect on those people that made your day a happy one, or showed you support and list them.)

1
2
3
4
5

THE BEST PART OF YOUR DAY?

(Before you go to bed, think about what part of your day made you happy and reflect on it.)

1
2
3
4
5

SOMETHING FUN THAT YOU ARE LOOKING FORWARD TO?

My Thoughts

LET'S BE GRATEFUL!

Day......................... Month........................... Year.........................

LIST 5 THINGS YOU ARE GRATEFUL FOR TODAY.

(Before doing anything today, reflect on things that you wake up feeling grateful about.)

1
2
3
4
5

WHAT DID YOU LEARN TODAY?

(What did you learn from your challenges today? What positive lesson came from the day?)

1
2
3
4
5

PEOPLE YOU ARE GRATEFUL FOR?

(Reflect on those people that made your day a happy one, or showed you support and list them.)

1
2
3
4
5

THE BEST PART OF YOUR DAY?

(Before you go to bed, think about what part of your day made you happy and reflect on it.)

1
2
3
4
5

SOMETHING FUN THAT YOU ARE LOOKING FORWARD TO?

My Thoughts

" The grateful mind is constantly fixated upon the best. Therefore, it tends to become the best. It takes the form or character from the best and will receive the best."

WALLACE D. WATTLES

LET'S BE GRATEFUL!

Day.......................... Month........................... Year..........................

LIST 5 THINGS YOU ARE GRATEFUL FOR TODAY.

(Before doing anything today, reflect on things that you wake up feeling grateful about.)

1
2
3
4
5

WHAT DID YOU LEARN TODAY?

(What did you learn from your challenges today? What positive lesson came from the day?)

1
2
3
4
5

PEOPLE YOU ARE GRATEFUL FOR?

(Reflect on those people that made your day a happy one, or showed you support and list them.)

1
2
3
4
5

THE BEST PART OF YOUR DAY?

(Before you go to bed, think about what part of your day made you happy and reflect on it.)

1
2
3
4
5

SOMETHING FUN THAT YOU ARE LOOKING FORWARD TO?

My Thoughts

LET'S BE GRATEFUL!

Day............................ Month............................ Year............................

LIST 5 THINGS YOU ARE GRATEFUL FOR TODAY.

(Before doing anything today, reflect on things that you wake up feeling grateful about.)

1
2
3
4
5

WHAT DID YOU LEARN TODAY?

(What did you learn from your challenges today? What positive lesson came from the day?)

1
2
3
4
5

PEOPLE YOU ARE GRATEFUL FOR?

(Reflect on those people that made your day a happy one, or showed you support and list them.)

1
2
3
4
5

THE BEST PART OF YOUR DAY?

(Before you go to bed, think about what part of your day made you happy and reflect on it.)

1
2
3
4
5

SOMETHING FUN THAT YOU ARE LOOKING FORWARD TO?

My Thoughts

LET'S BE GRATEFUL!

Day......................... Month........................... Year.........................

LIST 5 THINGS YOU ARE GRATEFUL FOR TODAY.

(Before doing anything today, reflect on things that you wake up feeling grateful about.)

1
2
3
4
5

WHAT DID YOU LEARN TODAY?

(What did you learn from your challenges today? What positive lesson came from the day?)

1
2
3
4
5

PEOPLE YOU ARE GRATEFUL FOR?

(Reflect on those people that made your day a happy one, or showed you support and list them.)

1
2
3
4
5

THE BEST PART OF YOUR DAY?

(Before you go to bed, think about what part of your day made you happy and reflect on it.)

1
2
3
4
5

SOMETHING FUN THAT YOU ARE LOOKING FORWARD TO?

My Thoughts

" To accomplish great things, we must not only act, but also dream; not only plan, but also believe."

ANATOLE FRANCE

LET'S BE GRATEFUL!

Day........................ Month.......................... Year........................

LIST 5 THINGS YOU ARE GRATEFUL FOR TODAY.

(Before doing anything today, reflect on things that you wake up feeling grateful about.)

1
2
3
4
5

WHAT DID YOU LEARN TODAY?

(What did you learn from your challenges today? What positive lesson came from the day?)

1
2
3
4
5

PEOPLE YOU ARE GRATEFUL FOR?

(Reflect on those people that made your day a happy one, or showed you support and list them.)

1
2
3
4
5

THE BEST PART OF YOUR DAY?

(Before you go to bed, think about what part of your day made you happy and reflect on it.)

1
2
3
4
5

SOMETHING FUN THAT YOU ARE LOOKING FORWARD TO?

My Thoughts

LET'S BE GRATEFUL!

Day.......................... Month........................... Year..........................

LIST 5 THINGS YOU ARE GRATEFUL FOR TODAY.

(Before doing anything today, reflect on things that you wake up feeling grateful about.)

1
2
3
4
5

WHAT DID YOU LEARN TODAY?

(What did you learn from your challenges today? What positive lesson came from the day?)

1
2
3
4
5

PEOPLE YOU ARE GRATEFUL FOR?

(Reflect on those people that made your day a happy one, or showed you support and list them.)

1
2
3
4
5

THE BEST PART OF YOUR DAY?

(Before you go to bed, think about what part of your day made you happy and reflect on it.)

1
2
3
4
5

SOMETHING FUN THAT YOU ARE LOOKING FORWARD TO?

My Thoughts

LET'S BE GRATEFUL!

Day.......................... Month............................ Year..........................

LIST 5 THINGS YOU ARE GRATEFUL FOR TODAY.

(Before doing anything today, reflect on things that you wake up feeling grateful about.)

1
2
3
4
5

WHAT DID YOU LEARN TODAY?

(What did you learn from your challenges today? What positive lesson came from the day?)

1
2
3
4
5

PEOPLE YOU ARE GRATEFUL FOR?

(Reflect on those people that made your day a happy one, or showed you support and list them.)

1
2
3
4
5

THE BEST PART OF YOUR DAY?

(Before you go to bed, think about what part of your day made you happy and reflect on it.)

1
2
3
4
5

SOMETHING FUN THAT YOU ARE LOOKING FORWARD TO?

My Thoughts

"When one door of happiness closes, another opens; but often we look so long at the closed door that we do not see the one which has been opened for us."

HELEN KELLER

LET'S BE GRATEFUL!

Day............................ Month............................ Year............................

LIST 5 THINGS YOU ARE GRATEFUL FOR TODAY.

(Before doing anything today, reflect on things that you wake up feeling grateful about.)

1
2
3
4
5

WHAT DID YOU LEARN TODAY?

(What did you learn from your challenges today? What positive lesson came from the day?)

1
2
3
4
5

PEOPLE YOU ARE GRATEFUL FOR?

(Reflect on those people that made your day a happy one, or showed you support and list them.)

1
2
3
4
5

THE BEST PART OF YOUR DAY?

(Before you go to bed, think about what part of your day made you happy and reflect on it.)

1
2
3
4
5

SOMETHING FUN THAT YOU ARE LOOKING FORWARD TO?

My Thoughts

LET'S BE GRATEFUL!

Day........................... Month........................... Year...........................

LIST 5 THINGS YOU ARE GRATEFUL FOR TODAY.

(Before doing anything today, reflect on things that you wake up feeling grateful about.)

1
2
3
4
5

WHAT DID YOU LEARN TODAY?

(What did you learn from your challenges today? What positive lesson came from the day?)

1
2
3
4
5

PEOPLE YOU ARE GRATEFUL FOR?

(Reflect on those people that made your day a happy one, or showed you support and list them.)

1
2
3
4
5

THE BEST PART OF YOUR DAY?

(Before you go to bed, think about what part of your day made you happy and reflect on it.)

1
2
3
4
5

SOMETHING FUN THAT YOU ARE LOOKING FORWARD TO?

My Thoughts

LET'S BE GRATEFUL!

Day........................... Month........................... Year...........................

LIST 5 THINGS YOU ARE GRATEFUL FOR TODAY.

(Before doing anything today, reflect on things that you wake up feeling grateful about.)

1
2
3
4
5

WHAT DID YOU LEARN TODAY?

(What did you learn from your challenges today? What positive lesson came from the day?)

1
2
3
4
5

PEOPLE YOU ARE GRATEFUL FOR?

(Reflect on those people that made your day a happy one, or showed you support and list them.)

1
2
3
4
5

THE BEST PART OF YOUR DAY?

(Before you go to bed, think about what part of your day made you happy and reflect on it.)

1
2
3
4
5

SOMETHING FUN THAT YOU ARE LOOKING FORWARD TO?

My Thoughts

"Being grateful all the time isn't easy. But it's when you least feel thankful that you are most in need of what gratitude can give you: perspective. Gratitude can transform any situation. It alters your vibration, moving you from negative energy to positive. It's the quickest, easiest most powerful way to effect change in your life — this I know for sure.

OPRAH WINFREY

LET'S BE GRATEFUL!

Day......................... Month........................... Year.........................

LIST 5 THINGS YOU ARE GRATEFUL FOR TODAY.

(Before doing anything today, reflect on things that you wake up feeling grateful about.)

1
2
3
4
5

WHAT DID YOU LEARN TODAY?

(What did you learn from your challenges today? What positive lesson came from the day?)

1
2
3
4
5

PEOPLE YOU ARE GRATEFUL FOR?

(Reflect on those people that made your day a happy one, or showed you support and list them.)

1
2
3
4
5

THE BEST PART OF YOUR DAY?

(Before you go to bed, think about what part of your day made you happy and reflect on it.)

1
2
3
4
5

SOMETHING FUN THAT YOU ARE LOOKING FORWARD TO?

My Thoughts

LET'S BE GRATEFUL!

Day......................... Month........................... Year...........................

LIST 5 THINGS YOU ARE GRATEFUL FOR TODAY.

(Before doing anything today, reflect on things that you wake up feeling grateful about.)

1
2
3
4
5

WHAT DID YOU LEARN TODAY?

(What did you learn from your challenges today? What positive lesson came from the day?)

1
2
3
4
5

PEOPLE YOU ARE GRATEFUL FOR?

(Reflect on those people that made your day a happy one, or showed you support and list them.)

1
2
3
4
5

THE BEST PART OF YOUR DAY?

(Before you go to bed, think about what part of your day made you happy and reflect on it.)

1
2
3
4
5

SOMETHING FUN THAT YOU ARE LOOKING FORWARD TO?

My Thoughts

LET'S BE GRATEFUL!

Day......................... Month.......................... Year..........................

LIST 5 THINGS YOU ARE GRATEFUL FOR TODAY.

(Before doing anything today, reflect on things that you wake up feeling grateful about.)

1

2

3

4

5

WHAT DID YOU LEARN TODAY?

(What did you learn from your challenges today? What positive lesson came from the day?)

1

2

3

4

5

PEOPLE YOU ARE GRATEFUL FOR?

(Reflect on those people that made your day a happy one, or showed you support and list them.)

1

2

3

4

5

THE BEST PART OF YOUR DAY?

(Before you go to bed, think about what part of your day made you happy and reflect on it.)

1

2

3

4

5

SOMETHING FUN THAT YOU ARE LOOKING FORWARD TO?

My Thoughts

"Be thankful for what you have, you'll end up having more. If you concentrate on what you don't have, you will never ever have enough."

OPRAH WINFREY

LET'S BE GRATEFUL!

Day......................... Month........................... Year...........................

LIST 5 THINGS YOU ARE GRATEFUL FOR TODAY.

(Before doing anything today, reflect on things that you wake up feeling grateful about.)

1
2
3
4
5

WHAT DID YOU LEARN TODAY?

(What did you learn from your challenges today? What positive lesson came from the day?)

1
2
3
4
5

PEOPLE YOU ARE GRATEFUL FOR?

(Reflect on those people that made your day a happy one, or showed you support and list them.)

1
2
3
4
5

THE BEST PART OF YOUR DAY?

(Before you go to bed, think about what part of your day made you happy and reflect on it.)

1
2
3
4
5

SOMETHING FUN THAT YOU ARE LOOKING FORWARD TO?

My Thoughts

LET'S BE GRATEFUL!

| Day.......................... Month.......................... Year.......................... |

LIST 5 THINGS YOU ARE GRATEFUL FOR TODAY.

(Before doing anything today, reflect on things that you wake up feeling grateful about.)

1
2
3
4
5

WHAT DID YOU LEARN TODAY?

(What did you learn from your challenges today? What positive lesson came from the day?)

1
2
3
4
5

PEOPLE YOU ARE GRATEFUL FOR?

(Reflect on those people that made your day a happy one, or showed you support and list them.)

1
2
3
4
5

THE BEST PART OF YOUR DAY?

(Before you go to bed, think about what part of your day made you happy and reflect on it.)

1
2
3
4
5

SOMETHING FUN THAT YOU ARE LOOKING FORWARD TO?

My Thoughts

LET'S BE GRATEFUL!

Day........................ Month.......................... Year..........................

LIST 5 THINGS YOU ARE GRATEFUL FOR TODAY.

(Before doing anything today, reflect on things that you wake up feeling grateful about.)

1
2
3
4
5

WHAT DID YOU LEARN TODAY?

(What did you learn from your challenges today? What positive lesson came from the day?)

1
2
3
4
5

PEOPLE YOU ARE GRATEFUL FOR?

(Reflect on those people that made your day a happy one, or showed you support and list them.)

1
2
3
4
5

THE BEST PART OF YOUR DAY?

(Before you go to bed, think about what part of your day made you happy and reflect on it.)

1
2
3
4
5

SOMETHING FUN THAT YOU ARE LOOKING FORWARD TO?

My Thoughts

"As soon as you start to feel differently about what you already have, you will start to attract more of the good things, more of the things you can be grateful for."

JOE VITALE

LET'S BE GRATEFUL!

Day......................... Month.......................... Year...........................

LIST 5 THINGS YOU ARE GRATEFUL FOR TODAY.

(Before doing anything today, reflect on things that you wake up feeling grateful about.)

1
2
3
4
5

WHAT DID YOU LEARN TODAY?

(What did you learn from your challenges today? What positive lesson came from the day?)

1
2
3
4
5

PEOPLE YOU ARE GRATEFUL FOR?

(Reflect on those people that made your day a happy one, or showed you support and list them.)

1
2
3
4
5

THE BEST PART OF YOUR DAY?

(Before you go to bed, think about what part of your day made you happy and reflect on it.)

1
2
3
4
5

SOMETHING FUN THAT YOU ARE LOOKING FORWARD TO?

My Thoughts

LET'S BE GRATEFUL!

Day......................... Month........................... Year...........................

LIST 5 THINGS YOU ARE GRATEFUL FOR TODAY.

(Before doing anything today, reflect on things that you wake up feeling grateful about.)

1
2
3
4
5

WHAT DID YOU LEARN TODAY?

(What did you learn from your challenges today? What positive lesson came from the day?)

1
2
3
4
5

PEOPLE YOU ARE GRATEFUL FOR?

(Reflect on those people that made your day a happy one, or showed you support and list them.)

1
2
3
4
5

THE BEST PART OF YOUR DAY?

(Before you go to bed, think about what part of your day made you happy and reflect on it.)

1
2
3
4
5

SOMETHING FUN THAT YOU ARE LOOKING FORWARD TO?

My Thoughts

LET'S BE GRATEFUL!

Day.......................... Month........................... Year........................

LIST 5 THINGS YOU ARE GRATEFUL FOR TODAY.

(Before doing anything today, reflect on things that you wake up feeling grateful about.)

1
2
3
4
5

WHAT DID YOU LEARN TODAY?

(What did you learn from your challenges today? What positive lesson came from the day?)

1
2
3
4
5

PEOPLE YOU ARE GRATEFUL FOR?

(Reflect on those people that made your day a happy one, or showed you support and list them.)

1
2
3
4
5

THE BEST PART OF YOUR DAY?

(Before you go to bed, think about what part of your day made you happy and reflect on it.)

1
2
3
4
5

SOMETHING FUN THAT YOU ARE LOOKING FORWARD TO?

My Thoughts

"Gratitude is an attitude that hooks us up to our source of supply. And the more grateful you are, the closer you become to your maker, to the architect of the universe, to the spiritual core of your being. It's a phenomenal lesson."

BOB PROCTOR

LET'S BE GRATEFUL!

Day.......................... Month........................... Year...........................

LIST 5 THINGS YOU ARE GRATEFUL FOR TODAY.

(Before doing anything today, reflect on things that you wake up feeling grateful about.)

1
2
3
4
5

WHAT DID YOU LEARN TODAY?

(What did you learn from your challenges today? What positive lesson came from the day?)

1
2
3
4
5

PEOPLE YOU ARE GRATEFUL FOR?

(Reflect on those people that made your day a happy one, or showed you support and list them.)

1
2
3
4
5

THE BEST PART OF YOUR DAY?

(Before you go to bed, think about what part of your day made you happy and reflect on it.)

1
2
3
4
5

SOMETHING FUN THAT YOU ARE LOOKING FORWARD TO?

My Thoughts

LET'S BE GRATEFUL!

Day.......................... Month.......................... Year..........................

LIST 5 THINGS YOU ARE GRATEFUL FOR TODAY.

(Before doing anything today, reflect on things that you wake up feeling grateful about.)

1
2
3
4
5

WHAT DID YOU LEARN TODAY?

(What did you learn from your challenges today? What positive lesson came from the day?)

1
2
3
4
5

PEOPLE YOU ARE GRATEFUL FOR?

(Reflect on those people that made your day a happy one, or showed you support and list them.)

1
2
3
4
5

THE BEST PART OF YOUR DAY?

(Before you go to bed, think about what part of your day made you happy and reflect on it.)

1
2
3
4
5

SOMETHING FUN THAT YOU ARE LOOKING FORWARD TO?

My Thoughts

LET'S BE GRATEFUL!

Day........................... Month........................... Year...........................

LIST 5 THINGS YOU ARE GRATEFUL FOR TODAY.

(Before doing anything today, reflect on things that you wake up feeling grateful about.)

1
2
3
4
5

WHAT DID YOU LEARN TODAY?

(What did you learn from your challenges today? What positive lesson came from the day?)

1
2
3
4
5

PEOPLE YOU ARE GRATEFUL FOR?

(Reflect on those people that made your day a happy one, or showed you support and list them.)

1
2
3
4
5

THE BEST PART OF YOUR DAY?

(Before you go to bed, think about what part of your day made you happy and reflect on it.)

1
2
3
4
5

SOMETHING FUN THAT YOU ARE LOOKING FORWARD TO?

My Thoughts

Some days the awareness of the sanctity and sacredness of life brings me to my knees with gratitude. I'm still trying to wrap my head around the idea that the little girl from Mississipi who grew up holding her nose in an outhouse now flies on her own plane — my own plane! — to Africa to help girls who grew up like her.

OPRAH WINFREY

LET'S BE GRATEFUL!

Day.......................... Month........................... Year..........................

LIST 5 THINGS YOU ARE GRATEFUL FOR TODAY.

(Before doing anything today, reflect on things that you wake up feeling grateful about.)

1
2
3
4
5

WHAT DID YOU LEARN TODAY?

(What did you learn from your challenges today? What positive lesson came from the day?)

1
2
3
4
5

PEOPLE YOU ARE GRATEFUL FOR?

(Reflect on those people that made your day a happy one, or showed you support and list them.)

1
2
3
4
5

THE BEST PART OF YOUR DAY?

(Before you go to bed, think about what part of your day made you happy and reflect on it.)

1
2
3
4
5

SOMETHING FUN THAT YOU ARE LOOKING FORWARD TO?

My Thoughts

LET'S BE GRATEFUL!

Day......................... Month........................... Year.........................

LIST 5 THINGS YOU ARE GRATEFUL FOR TODAY.

(Before doing anything today, reflect on things that you wake up feeling grateful about.)

1
2
3
4
5

WHAT DID YOU LEARN TODAY?

(What did you learn from your challenges today? What positive lesson came from the day?)

1
2
3
4
5

PEOPLE YOU ARE GRATEFUL FOR?

(Reflect on those people that made your day a happy one, or showed you support and list them.)

1
2
3
4
5

THE BEST PART OF YOUR DAY?

(Before you go to bed, think about what part of your day made you happy and reflect on it.)

1
2
3
4
5

SOMETHING FUN THAT YOU ARE LOOKING FORWARD TO?

My Thoughts

LET'S BE GRATEFUL!

Day........................... Month........................... Year...........................

LIST 5 THINGS YOU ARE GRATEFUL FOR TODAY.

(Before doing anything today, reflect on things that you wake up feeling grateful about.)

1
2
3
4
5

WHAT DID YOU LEARN TODAY?

(What did you learn from your challenges today? What positive lesson came from the day?)

1
2
3
4
5

PEOPLE YOU ARE GRATEFUL FOR?

(Reflect on those people that made your day a happy one, or showed you support and list them.)

1
2
3
4
5

THE BEST PART OF YOUR DAY?

(Before you go to bed, think about what part of your day made you happy and reflect on it.)

1
2
3
4
5

SOMETHING FUN THAT YOU ARE LOOKING FORWARD TO?

My Thoughts

"What are the things you are grateful for? Feel the gratitude… focus on what you have right now that you are grateful for."

UNKNOWN

LET'S BE GRATEFUL!

Day............................ Month............................ Year............................

LIST 5 THINGS YOU ARE GRATEFUL FOR TODAY.

(Before doing anything today, reflect on things that you wake up feeling grateful about.)

1
2
3
4
5

WHAT DID YOU LEARN TODAY?

(What did you learn from your challenges today? What positive lesson came from the day?)

1
2
3
4
5

PEOPLE YOU ARE GRATEFUL FOR?

(Reflect on those people that made your day a happy one, or showed you support and list them.)

1
2
3
4
5

THE BEST PART OF YOUR DAY?

(Before you go to bed, think about what part of your day made you happy and reflect on it.)

1
2
3
4
5

SOMETHING FUN THAT YOU ARE LOOKING FORWARD TO?

My Thoughts

LET'S BE GRATEFUL!

Day.......................... Month........................... Year..........................

LIST 5 THINGS YOU ARE GRATEFUL FOR TODAY.

(Before doing anything today, reflect on things that you wake up feeling grateful about.)

1
2
3
4
5

WHAT DID YOU LEARN TODAY?

(What did you learn from your challenges today? What positive lesson came from the day?)

1
2
3
4
5

PEOPLE YOU ARE GRATEFUL FOR?

(Reflect on those people that made your day a happy one, or showed you support and list them.)

1
2
3
4
5

THE BEST PART OF YOUR DAY?

(Before you go to bed, think about what part of your day made you happy and reflect on it.)

1
2
3
4
5

SOMETHING FUN THAT YOU ARE LOOKING FORWARD TO?

My Thoughts

LET'S BE GRATEFUL!

Day......................... Month........................... Year...........................

LIST 5 THINGS YOU ARE GRATEFUL FOR TODAY.

(Before doing anything today, reflect on things that you wake up feeling grateful about.)

1
2
3
4
5

WHAT DID YOU LEARN TODAY?

(What did you learn from your challenges today? What positive lesson came from the day?)

1
2
3
4
5

PEOPLE YOU ARE GRATEFUL FOR?

(Reflect on those people that made your day a happy one, or showed you support and list them.)

1
2
3
4
5

THE BEST PART OF YOUR DAY?

(Before you go to bed, think about what part of your day made you happy and reflect on it.)

1
2
3
4
5

SOMETHING FUN THAT YOU ARE LOOKING FORWARD TO?

My Thoughts

"Always be a first-rate version of yourself, instead of a second-rate version of somebody else."

JUDY GARLAND

LET'S BE GRATEFUL!

Day......................... Month........................... Year.........................

LIST 5 THINGS YOU ARE GRATEFUL FOR TODAY.

(Before doing anything today, reflect on things that you wake up feeling grateful about.)

1
2
3
4
5

WHAT DID YOU LEARN TODAY?

(What did you learn from your challenges today? What positive lesson came from the day?)

1
2
3
4
5

PEOPLE YOU ARE GRATEFUL FOR?

(Reflect on those people that made your day a happy one, or showed you support and list them.)

1
2
3
4
5

THE BEST PART OF YOUR DAY?

(Before you go to bed, think about what part of your day made you happy and reflect on it.)

1
2
3
4
5

SOMETHING FUN THAT YOU ARE LOOKING FORWARD TO?

My Thoughts

LET'S BE GRATEFUL!

Day.......................... Month........................... Year..........................

LIST 5 THINGS YOU ARE GRATEFUL FOR TODAY.

(Before doing anything today, reflect on things that you wake up feeling grateful about.)

1
2
3
4
5

WHAT DID YOU LEARN TODAY?

(What did you learn from your challenges today? What positive lesson came from the day?)

1
2
3
4
5

PEOPLE YOU ARE GRATEFUL FOR?

(Reflect on those people that made your day a happy one, or showed you support and list them.)

1
2
3
4
5

THE BEST PART OF YOUR DAY?

(Before you go to bed, think about what part of your day made you happy and reflect on it.)

1
2
3
4
5

SOMETHING FUN THAT YOU ARE LOOKING FORWARD TO?

My Thoughts

LET'S BE GRATEFUL!

Day........................ Month.......................... Year...........................

LIST 5 THINGS YOU ARE GRATEFUL FOR TODAY.

(Before doing anything today, reflect on things that you wake up feeling grateful about.)

1
2
3
4
5

WHAT DID YOU LEARN TODAY?

(What did you learn from your challenges today? What positive lesson came from the day?)

1
2
3
4
5

PEOPLE YOU ARE GRATEFUL FOR?

(Reflect on those people that made your day a happy one, or showed you support and list them.)

1
2
3
4
5

THE BEST PART OF YOUR DAY?

(Before you go to bed, think about what part of your day made you happy and reflect on it.)

1
2
3
4
5

SOMETHING FUN THAT YOU ARE LOOKING FORWARD TO?

My Thoughts

"When you realize your potential to feel good, you will ask no one to be different in order for you to feel good."

UNKNOWN

LET'S BE GRATEFUL!

Day......................... Month........................... Year..........................

LIST 5 THINGS YOU ARE GRATEFUL FOR TODAY.

(Before doing anything today, reflect on things that you wake up feeling grateful about.)

1
2
3
4
5

WHAT DID YOU LEARN TODAY?

(What did you learn from your challenges today? What positive lesson came from the day?)

1
2
3
4
5

PEOPLE YOU ARE GRATEFUL FOR?

(Reflect on those people that made your day a happy one, or showed you support and list them.)

1
2
3
4
5

THE BEST PART OF YOUR DAY?

(Before you go to bed, think about what part of your day made you happy and reflect on it.)

1
2
3
4
5

SOMETHING FUN THAT YOU ARE LOOKING FORWARD TO?

My Thoughts

LET'S BE GRATEFUL!

| Day.......................... Month.......................... Year.......................... |

LIST 5 THINGS YOU ARE GRATEFUL FOR TODAY.

(Before doing anything today, reflect on things that you wake up feeling grateful about.)

1
2
3
4
5

WHAT DID YOU LEARN TODAY?

(What did you learn from your challenges today? What positive lesson came from the day?)

1
2
3
4
5

PEOPLE YOU ARE GRATEFUL FOR?

(Reflect on those people that made your day a happy one, or showed you support and list them.)

1
2
3
4
5

THE BEST PART OF YOUR DAY?

(Before you go to bed, think about what part of your day made you happy and reflect on it.)

1
2
3
4
5

SOMETHING FUN THAT YOU ARE LOOKING FORWARD TO?

My Thoughts

LET'S BE GRATEFUL!

Day........................ Month........................ Year........................

LIST 5 THINGS YOU ARE GRATEFUL FOR TODAY.

(Before doing anything today, reflect on things that you wake up feeling grateful about.)

1
2
3
4
5

WHAT DID YOU LEARN TODAY?

(What did you learn from your challenges today? What positive lesson came from the day?)

1
2
3
4
5

PEOPLE YOU ARE GRATEFUL FOR?

(Reflect on those people that made your day a happy one, or showed you support and list them.)

1
2
3
4
5

THE BEST PART OF YOUR DAY?

(Before you go to bed, think about what part of your day made you happy and reflect on it.)

1
2
3
4
5

SOMETHING FUN THAT YOU ARE LOOKING FORWARD TO?

My Thoughts

" I live in a state of exhilarated contentment (my definition of happiness), fueled by a passion for everything I'm committed to: my work, my colleagues, my home, my gratitude for every breath taken in freedom and peace. And what makes it sweeter is knowing for sure that I created this happiness. It was my choice.

OPRAH WINFREY

LET'S BE GRATEFUL!

Day......................... Month......................... Year.........................

LIST 5 THINGS YOU ARE GRATEFUL FOR TODAY.

(Before doing anything today, reflect on things that you wake up feeling grateful about.)

1
2
3
4
5

WHAT DID YOU LEARN TODAY?

(What did you learn from your challenges today? What positive lesson came from the day?)

1
2
3
4
5

PEOPLE YOU ARE GRATEFUL FOR?

(Reflect on those people that made your day a happy one, or showed you support and list them.)

1
2
3
4
5

THE BEST PART OF YOUR DAY?

(Before you go to bed, think about what part of your day made you happy and reflect on it.)

1
2
3
4
5

SOMETHING FUN THAT YOU ARE LOOKING FORWARD TO?

My Thoughts

LET'S BE GRATEFUL!

Day........................... Month........................... Year...........................

LIST 5 THINGS YOU ARE GRATEFUL FOR TODAY.

(Before doing anything today, reflect on things that you wake up feeling grateful about.)

1
2
3
4
5

WHAT DID YOU LEARN TODAY?

(What did you learn from your challenges today? What positive lesson came from the day?)

1
2
3
4
5

PEOPLE YOU ARE GRATEFUL FOR?

(Reflect on those people that made your day a happy one, or showed you support and list them.)

1
2
3
4
5

THE BEST PART OF YOUR DAY?

(Before you go to bed, think about what part of your day made you happy and reflect on it.)

1
2
3
4
5

SOMETHING FUN THAT YOU ARE LOOKING FORWARD TO?

My Thoughts

LET'S BE GRATEFUL!

Day......................... Month.......................... Year.........................

LIST 5 THINGS YOU ARE GRATEFUL FOR TODAY.

(Before doing anything today, reflect on things that you wake up feeling grateful about.)

1
2
3
4
5

WHAT DID YOU LEARN TODAY?

(What did you learn from your challenges today? What positive lesson came from the day?)

1
2
3
4
5

PEOPLE YOU ARE GRATEFUL FOR?

(Reflect on those people that made your day a happy one, or showed you support and list them.)

1
2
3
4
5

THE BEST PART OF YOUR DAY?

(Before you go to bed, think about what part of your day made you happy and reflect on it.)

1
2
3
4
5

SOMETHING FUN THAT YOU ARE LOOKING FORWARD TO?

My Thoughts

"What you radiate outward in your thoughts, feelings, mental pictures and words, you attract into your life."

CATHERINE PONDER

LET'S BE GRATEFUL!

Day.......................... Month........................... Year..........................

LIST 5 THINGS YOU ARE GRATEFUL FOR TODAY.

(Before doing anything today, reflect on things that you wake up feeling grateful about.)

1
2
3
4
5

WHAT DID YOU LEARN TODAY?

(What did you learn from your challenges today? What positive lesson came from the day?)

1
2
3
4
5

PEOPLE YOU ARE GRATEFUL FOR?

(Reflect on those people that made your day a happy one, or showed you support and list them.)

1
2
3
4
5

THE BEST PART OF YOUR DAY?

(Before you go to bed, think about what part of your day made you happy and reflect on it.)

1
2
3
4
5

SOMETHING FUN THAT YOU ARE LOOKING FORWARD TO?

My Thoughts

LET'S BE GRATEFUL!

Day........................... Month.......................... Year..........................

LIST 5 THINGS YOU ARE GRATEFUL FOR TODAY.

(Before doing anything today, reflect on things that you wake up feeling grateful about.)

1
2
3
4
5

WHAT DID YOU LEARN TODAY?

(What did you learn from your challenges today? What positive lesson came from the day?)

1
2
3
4
5

PEOPLE YOU ARE GRATEFUL FOR?

(Reflect on those people that made your day a happy one, or showed you support and list them.)

1
2
3
4
5

THE BEST PART OF YOUR DAY?

(Before you go to bed, think about what part of your day made you happy and reflect on it.)

1
2
3
4
5

SOMETHING FUN THAT YOU ARE LOOKING FORWARD TO?

My Thoughts

LET'S BE GRATEFUL!

Day.......................... Month........................... Year..........................

LIST 5 THINGS YOU ARE GRATEFUL FOR TODAY.

(Before doing anything today, reflect on things that you wake up feeling grateful about.)

1
2
3
4
5

WHAT DID YOU LEARN TODAY?

(What did you learn from your challenges today? What positive lesson came from the day?)

1
2
3
4
5

PEOPLE YOU ARE GRATEFUL FOR?

(Reflect on those people that made your day a happy one, or showed you support and list them.)

1
2
3
4
5

THE BEST PART OF YOUR DAY?

(Before you go to bed, think about what part of your day made you happy and reflect on it.)

1
2
3
4
5

SOMETHING FUN THAT YOU ARE LOOKING FORWARD TO?

My Thoughts

"Man, alone, has the power to transform his thoughts into physical reality; man, alone, can dream and make his dreams come true."

NAPOLEON HILL

LET'S BE GRATEFUL!

Day........................ Month........................... Year..........................

LIST 5 THINGS YOU ARE GRATEFUL FOR TODAY.

(Before doing anything today, reflect on things that you wake up feeling grateful about.)

1
2
3
4
5

WHAT DID YOU LEARN TODAY?

(What did you learn from your challenges today? What positive lesson came from the day?)

1
2
3
4
5

PEOPLE YOU ARE GRATEFUL FOR?

(Reflect on those people that made your day a happy one, or showed you support and list them.)

1
2
3
4
5

THE BEST PART OF YOUR DAY?

(Before you go to bed, think about what part of your day made you happy and reflect on it.)

1
2
3
4
5

SOMETHING FUN THAT YOU ARE LOOKING FORWARD TO?

My Thoughts

LET'S BE GRATEFUL!

Day........................... Month............................ Year...........................

LIST 5 THINGS YOU ARE GRATEFUL FOR TODAY.

(Before doing anything today, reflect on things that you wake up feeling grateful about.)

1
2
3
4
5

WHAT DID YOU LEARN TODAY?

(What did you learn from your challenges today? What positive lesson came from the day?)

1
2
3
4
5

PEOPLE YOU ARE GRATEFUL FOR?

(Reflect on those people that made your day a happy one, or showed you support and list them.)

1
2
3
4
5

THE BEST PART OF YOUR DAY?

(Before you go to bed, think about what part of your day made you happy and reflect on it.)

1
2
3
4
5

SOMETHING FUN THAT YOU ARE LOOKING FORWARD TO?

My Thoughts

_____
_____
_____
_____
_____
_____
_____
_____
_____
_____
_____
_____
_____
_____
_____
_____
_____
_____
_____
_____
_____
_____
_____
_____
_____
_____
_____
_____

LET'S BE GRATEFUL!

Day........................ Month.......................... Year...........................

LIST 5 THINGS YOU ARE GRATEFUL FOR TODAY.

(Before doing anything today, reflect on things that you wake up feeling grateful about.)

1
2
3
4
5

WHAT DID YOU LEARN TODAY?

(What did you learn from your challenges today? What positive lesson came from the day?)

1
2
3
4
5

PEOPLE YOU ARE GRATEFUL FOR?

(Reflect on those people that made your day a happy one, or showed you support and list them.)

1
2
3
4
5

THE BEST PART OF YOUR DAY?

(Before you go to bed, think about what part of your day made you happy and reflect on it.)

1
2
3
4
5

SOMETHING FUN THAT YOU ARE LOOKING FORWARD TO?

My Thoughts

"All things are difficult before they are easy."

THOMAS FULLER

LET'S BE GRATEFUL!

Day........................... Month........................... Year...........................

LIST 5 THINGS YOU ARE GRATEFUL FOR TODAY.

(Before doing anything today, reflect on things that you wake up feeling grateful about.)

1
2
3
4
5

WHAT DID YOU LEARN TODAY?

(What did you learn from your challenges today? What positive lesson came from the day?)

1
2
3
4
5

PEOPLE YOU ARE GRATEFUL FOR?

(Reflect on those people that made your day a happy one, or showed you support and list them.)

1
2
3
4
5

THE BEST PART OF YOUR DAY?

(Before you go to bed, think about what part of your day made you happy and reflect on it.)

1
2
3
4
5

SOMETHING FUN THAT YOU ARE LOOKING FORWARD TO?

My Thoughts

LET'S BE GRATEFUL!

Day......................... Month........................... Year..........................

LIST 5 THINGS YOU ARE GRATEFUL FOR TODAY.

(Before doing anything today, reflect on things that you wake up feeling grateful about.)

1
2
3
4
5

WHAT DID YOU LEARN TODAY?

(What did you learn from your challenges today? What positive lesson came from the day?)

1
2
3
4
5

PEOPLE YOU ARE GRATEFUL FOR?

(Reflect on those people that made your day a happy one, or showed you support and list them.)

1
2
3
4
5

THE BEST PART OF YOUR DAY?

(Before you go to bed, think about what part of your day made you happy and reflect on it.)

1
2
3
4
5

SOMETHING FUN THAT YOU ARE LOOKING FORWARD TO?

My Thoughts

LET'S BE GRATEFUL!

Day........................ Month........................ Year........................

LIST 5 THINGS YOU ARE GRATEFUL FOR TODAY.

(Before doing anything today, reflect on things that you wake up feeling grateful about.)

1
2
3
4
5

WHAT DID YOU LEARN TODAY?

(What did you learn from your challenges today? What positive lesson came from the day?)

1
2
3
4
5

PEOPLE YOU ARE GRATEFUL FOR?

(Reflect on those people that made your day a happy one, or showed you support and list them.)

1
2
3
4
5

THE BEST PART OF YOUR DAY?

(Before you go to bed, think about what part of your day made you happy and reflect on it.)

1
2
3
4
5

SOMETHING FUN THAT YOU ARE LOOKING FORWARD TO?

My Thoughts

"Wherever you are in your journey, I hope you, too, will keep encountering challenges. It is a blessing to be able to survive them, to be able to keep putting one foot in front of the other — to be in a position to make the climb up life's mountain, knowing that the summit still lies ahead. And every experience is a valuable teacher.

OPRAH WINFREY

LET'S BE GRATEFUL!

Day........................... Month............................ Year...........................

LIST 5 THINGS YOU ARE GRATEFUL FOR TODAY.

(Before doing anything today, reflect on things that you wake up feeling grateful about.)

1
2
3
4
5

WHAT DID YOU LEARN TODAY?

(What did you learn from your challenges today? What positive lesson came from the day?)

1
2
3
4
5

PEOPLE YOU ARE GRATEFUL FOR?

(Reflect on those people that made your day a happy one, or showed you support and list them.)

1
2
3
4
5

THE BEST PART OF YOUR DAY?

(Before you go to bed, think about what part of your day made you happy and reflect on it.)

1
2
3
4
5

SOMETHING FUN THAT YOU ARE LOOKING FORWARD TO?

My Thoughts

LET'S BE GRATEFUL!

Day............................ Month............................ Year............................

LIST 5 THINGS YOU ARE GRATEFUL FOR TODAY.

(Before doing anything today, reflect on things that you wake up feeling grateful about.)

1
2
3
4
5

WHAT DID YOU LEARN TODAY?

(What did you learn from your challenges today? What positive lesson came from the day?)

1
2
3
4
5

PEOPLE YOU ARE GRATEFUL FOR?

(Reflect on those people that made your day a happy one, or showed you support and list them.)

1
2
3
4
5

THE BEST PART OF YOUR DAY?

(Before you go to bed, think about what part of your day made you happy and reflect on it.)

1
2
3
4
5

SOMETHING FUN THAT YOU ARE LOOKING FORWARD TO?

My Thoughts

LET'S BE GRATEFUL!

| Day.......................... Month............................ Year........................... |

LIST 5 THINGS YOU ARE GRATEFUL FOR TODAY.

(Before doing anything today, reflect on things that you wake up feeling grateful about.)

1.
2.
3.
4.
5.

WHAT DID YOU LEARN TODAY?

(What did you learn from your challenges today? What positive lesson came from the day?)

1.
2.
3.
4.
5.

PEOPLE YOU ARE GRATEFUL FOR?

(Reflect on those people that made your day a happy one, or showed you support and list them.)

1.
2.
3.
4.
5.

THE BEST PART OF YOUR DAY?

(Before you go to bed, think about what part of your day made you happy and reflect on it.)

1.
2.
3.
4.
5.

SOMETHING FUN THAT YOU ARE LOOKING FORWARD TO?

My Thoughts

" Man, alone, has the power to transform his thoughts into physical reality; man, alone, can dream and make his dreams come true."

NAPOLEON HILL

LET'S BE GRATEFUL!

Day........................... Month........................... Year...........................

LIST 5 THINGS YOU ARE GRATEFUL FOR TODAY.

(Before doing anything today, reflect on things that you wake up feeling grateful about.)

1
2
3
4
5

WHAT DID YOU LEARN TODAY?

(What did you learn from your challenges today? What positive lesson came from the day?)

1
2
3
4
5

PEOPLE YOU ARE GRATEFUL FOR?

(Reflect on those people that made your day a happy one, or showed you support and list them.)

1
2
3
4
5

THE BEST PART OF YOUR DAY?

(Before you go to bed, think about what part of your day made you happy and reflect on it.)

1
2
3
4
5

SOMETHING FUN THAT YOU ARE LOOKING FORWARD TO?

My Thoughts

LET'S BE GRATEFUL!

Day........................... Month........................... Year...........................

LIST 5 THINGS YOU ARE GRATEFUL FOR TODAY.

(Before doing anything today, reflect on things that you wake up feeling grateful about.)

1
2
3
4
5

WHAT DID YOU LEARN TODAY?

(What did you learn from your challenges today? What positive lesson came from the day?)

1
2
3
4
5

PEOPLE YOU ARE GRATEFUL FOR?

(Reflect on those people that made your day a happy one, or showed you support and list them.)

1
2
3
4
5

THE BEST PART OF YOUR DAY?

(Before you go to bed, think about what part of your day made you happy and reflect on it.)

1
2
3
4
5

SOMETHING FUN THAT YOU ARE LOOKING FORWARD TO?

My Thoughts

LET'S BE GRATEFUL!

Day............................ Month............................ Year............................

LIST 5 THINGS YOU ARE GRATEFUL FOR TODAY.

(Before doing anything today, reflect on things that you wake up feeling grateful about.)

1
2
3
4
5

WHAT DID YOU LEARN TODAY?

(What did you learn from your challenges today? What positive lesson came from the day?)

1
2
3
4
5

PEOPLE YOU ARE GRATEFUL FOR?

(Reflect on those people that made your day a happy one, or showed you support and list them.)

1
2
3
4
5

THE BEST PART OF YOUR DAY?

(Before you go to bed, think about what part of your day made you happy and reflect on it.)

1
2
3
4
5

SOMETHING FUN THAT YOU ARE LOOKING FORWARD TO?

My Thoughts

"I can accept failure, everyone fails at something. But I can't accept not trying."

MICHAEL JORDAN

LET'S BE GRATEFUL!

Day......................... Month.......................... Year..........................

LIST 5 THINGS YOU ARE GRATEFUL FOR TODAY.

(Before doing anything today, reflect on things that you wake up feeling grateful about.)

1
2
3
4
5

WHAT DID YOU LEARN TODAY?

(What did you learn from your challenges today? What positive lesson came from the day?)

1
2
3
4
5

PEOPLE YOU ARE GRATEFUL FOR?

(Reflect on those people that made your day a happy one, or showed you support and list them.)

1
2
3
4
5

THE BEST PART OF YOUR DAY?

(Before you go to bed, think about what part of your day made you happy and reflect on it.)

1
2
3
4
5

SOMETHING FUN THAT YOU ARE LOOKING FORWARD TO?

My Thoughts

LET'S BE GRATEFUL!

Day......................... Month........................... Year.........................

LIST 5 THINGS YOU ARE GRATEFUL FOR TODAY.

(Before doing anything today, reflect on things that you wake up feeling grateful about.)

1
2
3
4
5

WHAT DID YOU LEARN TODAY?

(What did you learn from your challenges today? What positive lesson came from the day?)

1
2
3
4
5

PEOPLE YOU ARE GRATEFUL FOR?

(Reflect on those people that made your day a happy one, or showed you support and list them.)

1
2
3
4
5

THE BEST PART OF YOUR DAY?

(Before you go to bed, think about what part of your day made you happy and reflect on it.)

1
2
3
4
5

SOMETHING FUN THAT YOU ARE LOOKING FORWARD TO?

My Thoughts

LET'S BE GRATEFUL!

Day......................... Month........................... Year.........................

LIST 5 THINGS YOU ARE GRATEFUL FOR TODAY.

(Before doing anything today, reflect on things that you wake up feeling grateful about.)

1
2
3
4
5

WHAT DID YOU LEARN TODAY?

(What did you learn from your challenges today? What positive lesson came from the day?)

1
2
3
4
5

PEOPLE YOU ARE GRATEFUL FOR?

(Reflect on those people that made your day a happy one, or showed you support and list them.)

1
2
3
4
5

THE BEST PART OF YOUR DAY?

(Before you go to bed, think about what part of your day made you happy and reflect on it.)

1
2
3
4
5

SOMETHING FUN THAT YOU ARE LOOKING FORWARD TO?

My Thoughts

"Learning is
a gift. Even
when pain is
your teacher."

MAYA WATSON

LET'S BE GRATEFUL!

Day........................ Month........................ Year........................

LIST 5 THINGS YOU ARE GRATEFUL FOR TODAY.

(Before doing anything today, reflect on things that you wake up feeling grateful about.)

1
2
3
4
5

WHAT DID YOU LEARN TODAY?

(What did you learn from your challenges today? What positive lesson came from the day?)

1
2
3
4
5

PEOPLE YOU ARE GRATEFUL FOR?

(Reflect on those people that made your day a happy one, or showed you support and list them.)

1
2
3
4
5

THE BEST PART OF YOUR DAY?

(Before you go to bed, think about what part of your day made you happy and reflect on it.)

1
2
3
4
5

SOMETHING FUN THAT YOU ARE LOOKING FORWARD TO?

My Thoughts

LET'S BE GRATEFUL!

Day........................... Month........................... Year...........................

LIST 5 THINGS YOU ARE GRATEFUL FOR TODAY.

(Before doing anything today, reflect on things that you wake up feeling grateful about.)

1
2
3
4
5

WHAT DID YOU LEARN TODAY?

(What did you learn from your challenges today? What positive lesson came from the day?)

1
2
3
4
5

PEOPLE YOU ARE GRATEFUL FOR?

(Reflect on those people that made your day a happy one, or showed you support and list them.)

1
2
3
4
5

THE BEST PART OF YOUR DAY?

(Before you go to bed, think about what part of your day made you happy and reflect on it.)

1
2
3
4
5

SOMETHING FUN THAT YOU ARE LOOKING FORWARD TO?

My Thoughts

LET'S BE GRATEFUL!

Day......................... Month............................ Year.........................

LIST 5 THINGS YOU ARE GRATEFUL FOR TODAY.

(Before doing anything today, reflect on things that you wake up feeling grateful about.)

1
2
3
4
5

WHAT DID YOU LEARN TODAY?

(What did you learn from your challenges today? What positive lesson came from the day?)

1
2
3
4
5

PEOPLE YOU ARE GRATEFUL FOR?

(Reflect on those people that made your day a happy one, or showed you support and list them.)

1
2
3
4
5

THE BEST PART OF YOUR DAY?

(Before you go to bed, think about what part of your day made you happy and reflect on it.)

1
2
3
4
5

SOMETHING FUN THAT YOU ARE LOOKING FORWARD TO?

My Thoughts

"I can be changed by what happened to me, but I refuse to be reduced by it."

LET'S BE GRATEFUL!

Day......................... Month......................... Year.........................

LIST 5 THINGS YOU ARE GRATEFUL FOR TODAY.

(Before doing anything today, reflect on things that you wake up feeling grateful about.)

1
2
3
4
5

WHAT DID YOU LEARN TODAY?

(What did you learn from your challenges today? What positive lesson came from the day?)

1
2
3
4
5

PEOPLE YOU ARE GRATEFUL FOR?

(Reflect on those people that made your day a happy one, or showed you support and list them.)

1
2
3
4
5

THE BEST PART OF YOUR DAY?

(Before you go to bed, think about what part of your day made you happy and reflect on it.)

1
2
3
4
5

SOMETHING FUN THAT YOU ARE LOOKING FORWARD TO?

My Thoughts

LET'S BE GRATEFUL!

| Day........................ Month........................... Year......................... |

LIST 5 THINGS YOU ARE GRATEFUL FOR TODAY.

(Before doing anything today, reflect on things that you wake up feeling grateful about.)

1
2
3
4
5

WHAT DID YOU LEARN TODAY?

(What did you learn from your challenges today? What positive lesson came from the day?)

1
2
3
4
5

PEOPLE YOU ARE GRATEFUL FOR?

(Reflect on those people that made your day a happy one, or showed you support and list them.)

1
2
3
4
5

THE BEST PART OF YOUR DAY?

(Before you go to bed, think about what part of your day made you happy and reflect on it.)

1
2
3
4
5

SOMETHING FUN THAT YOU ARE LOOKING FORWARD TO?

My Thoughts

LET'S BE GRATEFUL!

Day............................ Month............................ Year............................

LIST 5 THINGS YOU ARE GRATEFUL FOR TODAY.

(Before doing anything today, reflect on things that you wake up feeling grateful about.)

1
2
3
4
5

WHAT DID YOU LEARN TODAY?

(What did you learn from your challenges today? What positive lesson came from the day?)

1
2
3
4
5

PEOPLE YOU ARE GRATEFUL FOR?

(Reflect on those people that made your day a happy one, or showed you support and list them.)

1
2
3
4
5

THE BEST PART OF YOUR DAY?

(Before you go to bed, think about what part of your day made you happy and reflect on it.)

1
2
3
4
5

SOMETHING FUN THAT YOU ARE LOOKING FORWARD TO?

My Thoughts

"Nurture your mind with great thoughts, for you will never go any higher than you think."

BENJAMIN DISRAELI

LET'S BE GRATEFUL!

Day.......................... Month........................... Year...........................

LIST 5 THINGS YOU ARE GRATEFUL FOR TODAY.

(Before doing anything today, reflect on things that you wake up feeling grateful about.)

1
2
3
4
5

WHAT DID YOU LEARN TODAY?

(What did you learn from your challenges today? What positive lesson came from the day?)

1
2
3
4
5

PEOPLE YOU ARE GRATEFUL FOR?

(Reflect on those people that made your day a happy one, or showed you support and list them.)

1
2
3
4
5

THE BEST PART OF YOUR DAY?

(Before you go to bed, think about what part of your day made you happy and reflect on it.)

1
2
3
4
5

SOMETHING FUN THAT YOU ARE LOOKING FORWARD TO?

My Thoughts

LET'S BE GRATEFUL!

Day......................... Month........................... Year.........................

LIST 5 THINGS YOU ARE GRATEFUL FOR TODAY.

(Before doing anything today, reflect on things that you wake up feeling grateful about.)

1
2
3
4
5

WHAT DID YOU LEARN TODAY?

(What did you learn from your challenges today? What positive lesson came from the day?)

1
2
3
4
5

PEOPLE YOU ARE GRATEFUL FOR?

(Reflect on those people that made your day a happy one, or showed you support and list them.)

1
2
3
4
5

THE BEST PART OF YOUR DAY?

(Before you go to bed, think about what part of your day made you happy and reflect on it.)

1
2
3
4
5

SOMETHING FUN THAT YOU ARE LOOKING FORWARD TO?

My Thoughts

LET'S BE GRATEFUL!

Day........................... Month........................... Year...........................

LIST 5 THINGS YOU ARE GRATEFUL FOR TODAY.

(Before doing anything today, reflect on things that you wake up feeling grateful about.)

1
2
3
4
5

WHAT DID YOU LEARN TODAY?

(What did you learn from your challenges today? What positive lesson came from the day?)

1
2
3
4
5

PEOPLE YOU ARE GRATEFUL FOR?

(Reflect on those people that made your day a happy one, or showed you support and list them.)

1
2
3
4
5

THE BEST PART OF YOUR DAY?

(Before you go to bed, think about what part of your day made you happy and reflect on it.)

1
2
3
4
5

SOMETHING FUN THAT YOU ARE LOOKING FORWARD TO?

My Thoughts

"Whether you think you can or think you can't, either way you are right."

HENRY FORD

LET'S BE GRATEFUL!

Day......................... Month............................ Year............................

LIST 5 THINGS YOU ARE GRATEFUL FOR TODAY.

(Before doing anything today, reflect on things that you wake up feeling grateful about.)

1
2
3
4
5

WHAT DID YOU LEARN TODAY?

(What did you learn from your challenges today? What positive lesson came from the day?)

1
2
3
4
5

PEOPLE YOU ARE GRATEFUL FOR?

(Reflect on those people that made your day a happy one, or showed you support and list them.)

1
2
3
4
5

THE BEST PART OF YOUR DAY?

(Before you go to bed, think about what part of your day made you happy and reflect on it.)

1
2
3
4
5

SOMETHING FUN THAT YOU ARE LOOKING FORWARD TO?

My Thoughts

LET'S BE GRATEFUL!

Day......................... Month........................... Year...........................

LIST 5 THINGS YOU ARE GRATEFUL FOR TODAY.

(Before doing anything today, reflect on things that you wake up feeling grateful about.)

1
2
3
4
5

WHAT DID YOU LEARN TODAY?

(What did you learn from your challenges today? What positive lesson came from the day?)

1
2
3
4
5

PEOPLE YOU ARE GRATEFUL FOR?

(Reflect on those people that made your day a happy one, or showed you support and list them.)

1
2
3
4
5

THE BEST PART OF YOUR DAY?

(Before you go to bed, think about what part of your day made you happy and reflect on it.)

1
2
3
4
5

SOMETHING FUN THAT YOU ARE LOOKING FORWARD TO?

My Thoughts

LET'S BE GRATEFUL!

Day......................... Month........................... Year..........................

LIST 5 THINGS YOU ARE GRATEFUL FOR TODAY.

(Before doing anything today, reflect on things that you wake up feeling grateful about.)

1.
2.
3.
4.
5.

WHAT DID YOU LEARN TODAY?

(What did you learn from your challenges today? What positive lesson came from the day?)

1.
2.
3.
4.
5.

PEOPLE YOU ARE GRATEFUL FOR?

(Reflect on those people that made your day a happy one, or showed you support and list them.)

1.
2.
3.
4.
5.

THE BEST PART OF YOUR DAY?

(Before you go to bed, think about what part of your day made you happy and reflect on it.)

1.
2.
3.
4.
5.

SOMETHING FUN THAT YOU ARE LOOKING FORWARD TO?

My Thoughts

" Everything will be okay in the end.If it's not okay, it's not the end."

UNKNOWN

LET'S BE GRATEFUL!

Day........................ Month.......................... Year..........................

LIST 5 THINGS YOU ARE GRATEFUL FOR TODAY.

(Before doing anything today, reflect on things that you wake up feeling grateful about.)

1
2
3
4
5

WHAT DID YOU LEARN TODAY?

(What did you learn from your challenges today? What positive lesson came from the day?)

1
2
3
4
5

PEOPLE YOU ARE GRATEFUL FOR?

(Reflect on those people that made your day a happy one, or showed you support and list them.)

1
2
3
4
5

THE BEST PART OF YOUR DAY?

(Before you go to bed, think about what part of your day made you happy and reflect on it.)

1
2
3
4
5

SOMETHING FUN THAT YOU ARE LOOKING FORWARD TO?

My Thoughts

LET'S BE GRATEFUL!

Day............................ Month............................ Year............................

LIST 5 THINGS YOU ARE GRATEFUL FOR TODAY.

(Before doing anything today, reflect on things that you wake up feeling grateful about.)

1
2
3
4
5

WHAT DID YOU LEARN TODAY?

(What did you learn from your challenges today? What positive lesson came from the day?)

1
2
3
4
5

PEOPLE YOU ARE GRATEFUL FOR?

(Reflect on those people that made your day a happy one, or showed you support and list them.)

1
2
3
4
5

THE BEST PART OF YOUR DAY?

(Before you go to bed, think about what part of your day made you happy and reflect on it.)

1
2
3
4
5

SOMETHING FUN THAT YOU ARE LOOKING FORWARD TO?

My Thoughts

LET'S BE GRATEFUL!

| Day.......................... Month.......................... Year.......................... |

LIST 5 THINGS YOU ARE GRATEFUL FOR TODAY.

(Before doing anything today, reflect on things that you wake up feeling grateful about.)

1
2
3
4
5

WHAT DID YOU LEARN TODAY?

(What did you learn from your challenges today? What positive lesson came from the day?)

1
2
3
4
5

PEOPLE YOU ARE GRATEFUL FOR?

(Reflect on those people that made your day a happy one, or showed you support and list them.)

1
2
3
4
5

THE BEST PART OF YOUR DAY?

(Before you go to bed, think about what part of your day made you happy and reflect on it.)

1
2
3
4
5

SOMETHING FUN THAT YOU ARE LOOKING FORWARD TO?

My Thoughts

"A moment of gratitude makes a difference in your attitude."

LET'S BE GRATEFUL!

Day........................ Month.......................... Year..........................

LIST 5 THINGS YOU ARE GRATEFUL FOR TODAY.

(Before doing anything today, reflect on things that you wake up feeling grateful about.)

1
2
3
4
5

WHAT DID YOU LEARN TODAY?

(What did you learn from your challenges today? What positive lesson came from the day?)

1
2
3
4
5

PEOPLE YOU ARE GRATEFUL FOR?

(Reflect on those people that made your day a happy one, or showed you support and list them.)

1
2
3
4
5

THE BEST PART OF YOUR DAY?

(Before you go to bed, think about what part of your day made you happy and reflect on it.)

1
2
3
4
5

SOMETHING FUN THAT YOU ARE LOOKING FORWARD TO?

My Thoughts

LET'S BE GRATEFUL!

Day........................ Month.......................... Year.........................

LIST 5 THINGS YOU ARE GRATEFUL FOR TODAY.

(Before doing anything today, reflect on things that you wake up feeling grateful about.)

1
2
3
4
5

WHAT DID YOU LEARN TODAY?

(What did you learn from your challenges today? What positive lesson came from the day?)

1
2
3
4
5

PEOPLE YOU ARE GRATEFUL FOR?

(Reflect on those people that made your day a happy one, or showed you support and list them.)

1
2
3
4
5

THE BEST PART OF YOUR DAY?

(Before you go to bed, think about what part of your day made you happy and reflect on it.)

1
2
3
4
5

SOMETHING FUN THAT YOU ARE LOOKING FORWARD TO?

My Thoughts

LET'S BE GRATEFUL!

Day......................... Month........................... Year...........................

LIST 5 THINGS YOU ARE GRATEFUL FOR TODAY.

(Before doing anything today, reflect on things that you wake up feeling grateful about.)

1
2
3
4
5

WHAT DID YOU LEARN TODAY?

(What did you learn from your challenges today? What positive lesson came from the day?)

1
2
3
4
5

PEOPLE YOU ARE GRATEFUL FOR?

(Reflect on those people that made your day a happy one, or showed you support and list them.)

1
2
3
4
5

THE BEST PART OF YOUR DAY?

(Before you go to bed, think about what part of your day made you happy and reflect on it.)

1
2
3
4
5

SOMETHING FUN THAT YOU ARE LOOKING FORWARD TO?

My Thoughts

Gratitude Scriptures

1. Psalm 107:1 (NIV) - "Give thanks to the LORD, for he is good; his love endures forever."

2. 1 Thessalonians 5:18 (NIV) – "Give thanks in all circumstances, for this is God's will for you in Christ Jesus.

3. Colossians 4:2 (NIV) – "Devote yourselves to prayer, being watchful and thankful."

4. Colossians 3:15 (NIV) – "Let the peace of Christ rule in your hearts, since as members of one body you were called to peace. And be thankful."

5. Psalm 69:30 (NIV) – "I will praise God's name in song and glorify him with thanksgiving."

6. Ephesians 5:18-20 (ASV) – "Be filled with the Spirit; speaking one to another in psalms and hymns and spiritual songs, singing and making melody with your heart to the Lord; giving thanks always for all things in the name of our Lord Jesus Christ to God, even the Father."

7. Psalm 136:26 (AMP) – "Give thanks to the God of heaven, For His lovingkindness (graciousness, mercy, compassion) endures forever."

8. Psalm 106:1 (BRG) – "Praise ye the Lord. O give thanks unto the Lord; for he is good: for his mercy endureth forever."

9. Philippians 4:6-7 (CEB) – "Don't be anxious about anything; rather, bring up all of your requests to God in your prayers and petitions, along with giving thanks. Then the peace of God that exceeds all understanding will keep your hearts and minds safe in Christ Jesus."

10. John 6:11 (CEV) – "Jesus took the bread in his hands and gave thanks to God. Then he passed the bread to the people, and he did the same with the fish, until everyone had plenty to eat."

11. Psalm 28:7 (ESV) – "The Lord is my strength and my shield; in him my heart trusts, and I am helped; my heart exults, and with my song I give thanks to him."

12. Psalm 116:17 (ERV) – "I will give you a thank offering. I will call on the Lord's name."

13. Colossians 3:17 (EXB) – "Everything you do or say should be done to obey [or as a representative of; in the name of] the Lord Jesus. And in all you do, give thanks to God the Father through Jesus."

14. 2 Corinthians 9:15 (GNV) – "Thanks therefore be unto God for his unspeakable gift."

15. 1 Corinthians 15:57 (GW) – "Thank God that he gives us the victory through our Lord Jesus Christ."

16. Psalm 95:2 (GNT) – "Let us come before him with thanksgiving and sing joyful songs of praise."

17. Psalm 92:1 (KJV) – "It is a good thing to give thanks unto the LORD, and to sing praises unto thy name, O Most High."

18. Revelation 11:17 (ICB) - We give thanks to you, Lord God All-Powerful. You are the One who is and who was. We thank you because you have used your great power and have begun to rule!"

19. 1 Chronicles 29:13 (KJV) – "Now therefore, our God, we thank thee, and praise thy glorious name."

20. 2 Corinthians 2:14 (NIV) – "But thanks be to God, who always leads us as captives in Christ's triumphal procession and uses us to spread the aroma of the knowledge of him everywhere.!"

21. Psalm 105:1-2 (LEB) – "Give praise to the LORD, proclaim his name; make known among the nations what he has done. Sing to him, sing praise to him; tell of all his wonderful acts."

22. Psalm 30:4 (TLB) – "Oh, sing to him you saints of his; give thanks to his holy name."

23. Psalm 69:30 (MSG) – "Let me shout God's name with a praising song,

24. Let me tell his greatness in a prayer of thanks."

Gratitude Cards

I am grateful for enthusiasm	I am grateful for friends
I am grateful for support	I am grateful for dreams
I am grateful for courage	I am grateful for love
I am grateful for health	I am grateful for laughter
I am grateful for food on the table	I am grateful for the kindness of strangers
I am grateful for the beautiful sunrise	I am grateful for my strong arms
I am grateful for my eye sight	I am grateful for my feet
I am grateful for my voice	I am grateful for employment
I am grateful for payday	I am grateful for my pastor/ church
I am grateful for my family	I am grateful for my car
I am grateful for my passport	I am grateful for my strength

I am grateful for my drive	I am grateful for new clothes
I am thankful for supportive parents	I am grateful for my kids
I am grateful for my spouse	I am grateful for food on the table
I am grateful for my mind	I am grateful for my home
I am grateful for clean water	I am grateful for electricity
I am grateful for airplane	I am grateful for cellphone
I am grateful for computers	I am grateful for online dating
I am grateful for Netflix	I am grateful for Social Media
I am grateful for my pets	I am grateful for music
I am grateful for equality and diversity	I am grateful for movies
I am grateful for medication	I am grateful for the ability to read
I am grateful for breathing fresh air	I am grateful for a bed to sleep on
I am grateful for money in the bank	I am grateful for my mistakes
I am grateful for my challenges	I am grateful for freedom of speech

Made in the USA
Monee, IL
08 November 2019